I REFUSE TO FAIL

McDougal & Associates
Servants of Christ and Stewards of the
Mysteries of God

I REFUSE TO FAIL

by

Rev. Dr. Omolara Idowu

Published by:

Mcdougal & Associates
18896 Greenwell Springs Road
Greenwell Springs, LA 70739
www,ThePublishedWord.com

McDougal & Associates is dedicated to spreading the Gospel of the Lord Jesus Christ to as many people as possible in the shortest time possible.

ISBN: 978-1-950398-98-0

Printed on demand in the U.S., the U.K., Australia, and the UAE
For Worldwide Distribution

DEDICATION

I dedicate this book to every believer who is determined to win and not fail.

CONTENTS

Now thanks be unto God, which always causeth us to triumph in Christ, and maketh manifest the savour of his knowledge by us in every place.

— 2 Corinthians 2:14 KJV

FOREWORD BY BISHOP ABIOLA IDOWU

Life is all about the choices we make, and all that is needed for each of us to become a living star is included in God's plan of redemption. We are *"blessed with faithful Abraham"* (Galatians 3:9, KJV), so there is no room for failure in our lives whatsoever.

However, success is not automatic. We must make the right choices in order to succeed.

God said:

> *I call heaven and earth to record this day against you, that I have set before you life and death, blessing and cursing: therefore choose life, that both thou and thy seed may live.*   Deuteronomy 30:19, KJV

Yes, you must choose, and when you do make your choice, failure is not an option. In Christ, you are seated *"in heavenly places in Christ Jesus"* (Ephesians 2:6, KJV), *"far above all principality, and power, and might, and dominion"* (Ephesians 1:21, KJV). How can you possibly fail?

Think on this: There is a passion in every individual alive to become something. Nobody wants to remain stagnated or become redundant. Everyone wants health, fulfillment, and financial independence. Why is this true? Because there is something on the inside of each of us crying out for manifestation (see 2 Corinthians 4:7).

The treasure on the inside of you is the reason for the restlessness. Your inner man knows it is absurd to fail. But the treasure on the inside of you must be put to use to see the dream come to pass.

Dr. Omolara Idowu has brought God's Word into reality by sharing a life-changing truth with us in this book. There is unlimited potential inside of you. It's a lot like a blank check, and God is asking you to fill in the amount you want. Many don't write any amount because of the fear the check might bounce. Therefore, there is no dominion in their lives. Why? Because if the potential remains untapped, the person becomes redundant.

If we are *"without fault"* in God's eyes, then we have a place at the top (Ephesians 1:4). Never forget the fact that you didn't put this treasure there; God did. What He has put in you is on a mission to achieve His purpose for all of humanity.

Everyone comes in to this world with glory, but what happens to the glory in the inside depends on how we handle it (see Isaiah 43:7). David would have died in a sheepcote if he had never dared to fight Goliath. There are opportunities everywhere just waiting to be tapped so that we can become a star for the king and His Kingdom.

And it's not just about new ideas; it's also about executing the ideas you already have. If you're willing and determined, I'll see you at the top, for you must not and will not fail.

Don't just read this book; meditate on it and get the best out of it to the glory of God.

It is well!

Shalom!

Rt. Rev. Dr. Abiola Idowu

Presiding Bishop, CREPA Worldwide

INTRODUCTION

Beloved, it is what you know that makes you known. When you know it, you are victorious in life. God's commitment to you is His Covenant, and it is impossible for a covenant child of God to sink or to fail in life. Giving up in life is a negative mindset that no believer in Christ should have. There is no one on Earth who doesn't have a challenge, but you must refuse to give up. Life is not over yet. As Jesus was dying on the cross, He said:

IT IS FINISHED!   John 19:30, KJV

What is finished? Sickness is finished! Affliction is finished! Depression is finished! Pain is finished! And failure is finished! All in the name of Jesus. Yes, shout it today wherever you are: **IT IS FINISHED**!

As long as you have breath, your life is not yet finished. Numbers 23:23 tells us:

No magic spells can bind Jacob,
no incantations can hold back Israel.
People will look at Jacob and Israel and say,
"What a great thing has God done!"
Look, a people rising to its feet, stretch-ing like a lion,
a king-of-the-beasts, aroused,
Unsleeping, unresting until its hunt is over
and it's eaten and drunk its fill. (MSG)

Peter wrote to the early Church:

So, dear friends, don't let this one thing escape your notice: a single day counts like a thousand years to the Lord Yahweh, and a thousand years counts as one day. 2 Peter 3:8-9, TPT

It's not over, so don't give up. Refuse to fail! You were not destined for failure. You were destined for success. You were not destined for sickness. You were destined for healing. You were not destined for disappointment. You were destined for the best of everything.

Fail? Why would we ever utter that word? As a child of the living God, *I Refuse to Fail,* and you can refuse to fail too*!*

Rev. *Dr. Omolara Idowu*
Jacksonville, Florida

CHAPTER 1

QUICK, GOD, I NEED YOUR HELPING HAND!

"If you'll hold on to me for dear life," says God, "I'll get you out of any trouble. I'll give you the best of care if you'll only get to know and trust me. Call me and I'll answer, be at your side in bad times; I'll rescue you, then throw you a party. I'll give you a long life, give you a long drink of salvation!"

Psalm 91:15-16, MSG

What more could we ask for? God has not only promised us long life; He has promised to help us at every juncture of that life. He has specifically said that He will get us *"out*

of any trouble" and give us *"the best of care."*
Do you need help today? Your help is here.

These promises of God have been histori-
cally proven to be true:

> *Now the Spirit of God came upon*
> *Azariah the son of Oded. And he went*
> *out to meet Asa, and said to him: "Hear*
> *me, Asa, and all Judah and Benjamin.*
> *The Lord is with you while you are*
> *with Him. If you seek Him, He will be*
> *found by you; but if you forsake Him,*
> *He will forsake you. For a long time*
> *Israel has been without the true God,*
> *without a teaching priest, and without*
> *law; but when in their trouble they*
> *turned to the* LORD *God of Israel, and*
> *sought Him, He was found by them.*
> *And in those times there was no peace*
> *to the one who went out, nor to the one*
> *who came in, but great turmoil was on*
> *all the inhabitants of the lands. So na-*
> *tion was destroyed by nation, and city*
> *by city, for God troubled them with*
> *every adversity. But you, be strong and*

do not let your hands be weak, for your work shall be rewarded!"

2 Chronicles 15:1-7, NKJV

"Blessed is the man who trusts in the Lord,
And whose hope is the Lord.
For he shall be like a tree planted by the waters,
Which spreads out its roots by the river,
And will not fear when heat comes;
But its leaf will be green,
And will not be anxious in the year of drought,
Nor will cease from yielding fruit.

Jeremiah 17:7-8, NKJV

Our God is over all and is in control of all:

Thus says the Lord:
"Heaven is My throne,
And earth is My footstool.
Where is the house that you will build Me?
And where is the place of My rest?

Isaiah 66:1, NKJV

What, then, do we have to fear? God can and will even help a person who is already in the grave (see John 11:39-45). He did exactly that for Lazarus, so whatever your situation might be, God can handle it.

God rescued David from *"a horrible pit"*:

> *I waited patiently for the* LORD*;*
> *And He inclined to me,*
> *And heard my cry.*
> *He also brought me up out of a horrible pit,*
> *Out of the miry clay,*
> *And set my feet upon a rock,*
> *And established my steps.*
> *He has put a new song in my mouth—*
> *Praise to our God;*
> *Many will see it and fear,*
> *And will trust in the* LORD*.*
>
> Psalm 40:1-3, NKJV

In Elisha's time, a desperate widow called on God for help, and God gave her the miracle she needed (see 2 Kings 4:1-7). This woman was not only able to pay all her debts, keeping her sons out of debtor's prison; she had enough left over for them all to live on.

Poverty is no challenge for our God. *"He lifts the poor from the dust and the needy from the garbage dump"* and *"He sets them among princes, placing them in seats of honor"*:

> *The LORD makes some poor and others rich;*
> *he brings some down and lifts others up.*
> *He lifts the poor from the dust*
> *and the needy from the garbage dump.*
> *He sets them among princes,*
> *placing them in seats of honor.*
> *For all the earth is the LORD's, and he has set the world in order.*
> *He will protect his faithful ones,*
> *but the wicked will disappear in darkness.*
> *No one will succeed by strength alone.*
> 1 Samuel 2:7-9, NLT

Why would we turn to anyone or anything else in life when God has all the answers we need?

A horse is a vain hope for safety;
Neither shall it deliver any by its great
strength.
Behold, the eye of the LORD is on those
who fear Him,
On those who hope in His mercy,
To deliver their soul from death,
And to keep them alive in famine.
Our soul waits for the LORD;
He is our help and our shield.
For our heart shall rejoice in Him,
Because we have trusted in His holy
name.
Let Your mercy, O LORD, be upon us,
Just as we hope in You.
                              Psalm 33:17-22, NKJV

Your brother is not your help, and neither is your community. The greatest help anyone could ever hope to have is help from above:

My help comes from the LORD,
Who made heaven and earth.
                              Psalm 121:2, NKJV

22

How is all of this possible? Our God is making us more and more like Himself:

> *So all of us who have had that veil removed can see and reflect the glory of the Lord. And the Lord—who is the Spirit—makes us more and more like him as we are changed into his glorious image.* 2 Corinthians 3:18, NLT

Elisha encountered *"a great woman"* and found grace in her sight:

> *And it fell on a day, that Elisha passed to Shunem, where was a great woman; and she constrained him to eat bread. And so it was, that as oft as he passed by, he turned in thither to eat bread.* 2 Kings 4:8, KJV

As great as this woman was, she lacked something. She had no children, and her husband was old. All of that, however, was no problem for God. Elisha told her she would conceive and bear a son at the same time the next year, and it happened just as he had said (see verses 15-17). Nothing is hard for God. He said:

> *But they that wait upon the* Lord *shall renew their strength; they shall mount up with wings as eagles; they shall run, and not be weary; and they shall walk, and not faint.* Isaiah 40:31, KJV

Philip was sent by God to preach the Gospel to many places, but travel was so hard in those days that the Spirit picked him up and transported him miraculously:

> *When they came up out of the water, Philip was suddenly snatched up by the Spirit of the Lord and instantly carried away to the city of Ashdod, where he reappeared, preaching the gospel in that city. The man never saw Philip again. He returned to Ethiopia full of great joy. Philip, however, traveled on to all of the towns of that region, bringing*

them the good news, until he arrived at
Caesarea. Acts 8:39-40, TPT

Paul was another New Testament character who experienced many unusual miracles of God's intervention. Speaking of his own experience, he wrote:

And I know that this man (again, I'm not sure if he was still in his body or taken out of his body — God knows) was caught up in an ecstatic experience and brought into paradise, where he overheard many wondrous and inexpressible secrets that were so sacred that no mortal is permitted to repeat them.
2 Corinthians 12:3-4, TPT

He was not able to take personal credit for any of these things:

The extraordinary level of the revelations I've received is no reason for anyone to exalt me. For this is why a thorn in my flesh was given to me, the Adversary's

messenger sent to harass me, keeping me from becoming arrogant.
                    2 Corinthians 12:7, TPT

Paul sought God for this impediment to be removed, but God answered in this way:

But he answered me, "My grace is always more than enough for you, and my power finds its full expression through your weakness." So I will celebrate my weaknesses, for when I'm weak I sense more deeply the mighty power of Christ living in me. So I'm not defeated by my weakness, but delighted! For when I feel my weakness and endure mistreatment—when I'm surrounded with troubles on every side and face persecution because of my love for Christ—I am made yet stronger. For my weakness becomes a portal to God's power.
                    2 Corinthians 12:9-10, TPT

Paul prayed for the Ephesian believers:

I pray that you will continually experience the immeasurable greatness of God's power made available to you through faith. Then your lives will be an advertisement of this immense power as it works through you! This is the mighty power that was released when God raised Christ from the dead and exalted him to the place of highest honor and supreme authority in the heavenly realm! And now he is exalted as first above every ruler, authority, government, and realm of power in existence! He is gloriously enthroned over every name that is ever praised, not only in this age, but in the age that is coming! And he alone is the leader and source of everything needed in the church. God has put everything beneath the authority of Jesus Christ and has given him the highest rank above all others.

Ephesians 1:19-22, TPT

Paul summarized how these things were possible:

He raised us up with Christ the exalted One, and we ascended with him into the glorious perfection and authority of the heavenly realm, for we are now co-seated as one with Christ!

Ephesians 2:6, TPT

So the matchless and never-ending power of God is available to us today. How can we access His help? Here are some important keys:

1. Access God's Help By Expressing Your Humility

Through her humility, a woman of Canaan received healing for her demon-possessed daughter (see Matthew 15:21-28).

King Uzziah began his reign at the tender age of sixteen, and because of his humility, God blessed him:

God helped him in his wars against the Philistines, his battles with the Arabs of Gur, and his wars with the Meunites.

28

And he built structures on the walls of Jerusalem, designed by experts to protect those who shot arrows and hurled large stones from the towers and the corners of the wall. His fame spread far and wide, for the LORD gave him marvelous help, and he became very powerful.

2 Chronicles 26:14-15, NLT

Then, however, something terrible happened to Uzziah:

But when he had become powerful, he also became proud, which led to his downfall. He sinned against the LORD his God by entering the sanctuary of the LORD's Temple and personally burning incense on the incense altar. Azariah the high priest went in after him with eighty other priests of the LORD, all brave men. They confronted King Uzziah and said, "It is not for you, Uzziah, to burn incense to the LORD. That is the work of the priests alone, the descendants of Aaron who are set apart for this work.

Get out of the sanctuary, for you have sinned. The LORD *God will not honor you for this!"*

Uzziah, who was holding an incense burner, became furious. But as he was standing there raging at the priests before the incense altar in the LORD's *Temple, leprosy suddenly broke out on his forehead.*

When Azariah the high priest and all the other priests saw the leprosy, they rushed him out. And the king himself was eager to get out because the LORD *had struck him. So King Uzziah had leprosy until the day he died. He lived in isolation in a separate house, for he was excluded from the Temple of the* LORD. *His son Jotham was put in charge of the royal palace, and he governed the people of the land.*   2 Chronicles 26:16-21

This lesson is valid for people of all generations. Stay humble before God, and you will have access to His help at all times! Become proud and He will no longer hear your prayers!

2. ACCESS GOD'S HELP BY UNDERSTANDING THE STRENGTH OF OUR HELPER

The psalmist understood God's power:

A SONG OF THE STAIRWAY

I look up to the mountains and hills, longing for God's help.
But then I realize that our true help and protection come only from the LORD, our Creator who made the heavens and the earth. Psalm 121:1-2, TPT

You cannot do anything extraordinary by yourself, and you will never rise unassisted. The race is not to the swift:

I returned, and saw under the sun, that the race is not to the swift, nor the battle to the strong, neither yet bread to the wise, nor yet riches to men of under-standing, nor yet favour to men of skill;

31

> *but time and chance happeneth to them*
> *all.*   Ecclesiastes 9:11, KJV

Don't be so foolish as to think you can make it on your own. Understand the strength of our Helper!

3. ACCESS GOD'S HELP BY FOLLOWING THE STRATEGIES HE GIVES YOU

A great example of this was Joshua and the children of Israel as they approached the first major city in the Promised Land, Jericho:

> *Now the gates of Jericho were tightly shut because the people were afraid of the Israelites. No one was allowed to go out or in. But the LORD said to Joshua, "I have given you Jericho, its king, and all its strong warriors. You and your fighting men should march around the town once a day for six days. Seven priests will walk ahead of the Ark, each carrying a ram's horn. On the seventh*

day you are to march around the town seven times, with the priests blowing the horns. When you hear the priests give one long blast on the rams' horns, have all the people shout as loud as they can. Then the walls of the town will collapse, and the people can charge straight into the town."

So Joshua called together the priests and said, "Take up the Ark of the LORD's Covenant, and assign seven priests to walk in front of it, each carrying a ram's horn."　　Joshua 6:1-6, NLT

We know what happened, and it happened because Joshua put to work the exact strategy the Lord had shown him. Many believers, knowing that keys are for opening doors, are not quite sure why they don't seem to open walls too. Do with what God has given you as He instructs. The only One who can open ways where there is no way is God Himself. Keep Him on your side and working on your behalf by obeying His voice in all things.

4. ACCESS GOD'S HELP BY TRUSTING HIM WITH ALL YOUR HEART

Jeremiah expressed it this way:

> *Cursed is the one who trusts in human strength and the abilities of mere mortals.*
> *His very heart strays from the Eternal.*
> *He is like a little shrub in the desert that never grows;*
> *he will see no good thing come his way.*
> *He will live in a desert wasteland,*
> *a barren land of salt where no one lives.*
> *But blessed is the one who trusts in Me alone;*
> *the Eternal will be his confidence.*
> *He is like a tree planted by water,*
> *sending out its roots beside the stream.*
> *It does not fear the heat or even drought.*
> *Its leaves stay green and its fruit is dependable, no matter what it faces.*
>
> Jeremiah 17:5-8, VOICE

The wise King Solomon wrote:

*Trust in the L*ORD *with all your heart;*
do not depend on your own
understanding.
Don't be impressed with your own
wisdom.
*Instead, fear the L*ORD *and turn away*
from evil.
Then you will have healing for your
body
and strength for your bones.
                    Proverbs 3:5, and 7-8, NLT

Because of his trust in the goodness of God, Joshua was led to tell his people to shout at a specified moment, long before victory seemed assured in the natural:

The seventh time around, as the priests
sounded the long blast on their horns,
Joshua commanded the people, "Shout!
*For the L*ORD *has given you the town!"*
                            Joshua 6:16, NLT

Some might say, "I could never shout when people are trying to kill me." Others might have objected that they had been marching around the city for seven days already, and nothing had changed. Those fortified walls were still standing. But, because God had assured Joshua that he would indeed overcome this seemingly-impregnable city, he, in turn, could assure the people of the same. In that moment of faith, they saw those walls fallen. What do you see?

One of the easiest ways to trust God is by remembering His wonders of old. When we forget what He has done, we tend to go astray:

> *The children of Ephraim, being armed, and carrying bows, turned back in the day of battle.*
> *They kept not the covenant of God, and refused to walk in his law;*
> *Yea, they turned back and tempted God, and limited the Holy One of Israel.*
> *They remembered not his hand, nor the day when he delivered them from the enemy.*
>
> Psalm 78:9-10 and 41-42, KJV

Never stop trusting God, no matter what happens.

5. ACCESS GOD'S HELP BY PRAISING HIM IN ADVANCE

He [Jahaziel] said, "Listen, all you people of Judah and Jerusalem! Listen, King Jehoshaphat! This is what the LORD says: Do not be afraid! Don't be discouraged by this mighty army, for the battle is not yours, but God's. Tomorrow, march out against them. You will find them coming up through the ascent of Ziz at the end of the valley that opens into the wilderness of Jeruel. But you will not even need to fight. Take your positions; then stand still and watch the LORD's victory. He is with you, O people of Judah and Jerusalem. Do not be afraid or discouraged. Go out against them tomorrow, for the LORD is with you!"

After consulting the people, the king appointed singers to walk ahead of the *army, singing to the L*ORD *and praising him for his holy splendor. This is what they sang: "Give thanks to the L*ORD*; his faithful love endures forever!"*

2 Chronicles 20:15-17, and 21, NLT

It worked for King Jehoshaphat, and it will work for you too. When God shows you what He wants to do in your life, start praising Him from that moment on. If He said it, He will do it, so consider it done.

6. Access God's Help through the Holy Spirit

The Holy Spirit in us helps us to stay spiritually alert and awake. John the Baptist preached to the many who came out to hear him in his day:

"I baptize with water those who repent of their sins and turn to God. But someone is coming soon who is greater than I am—so much greater that I'm not worthy even to be his slave and carry

his sandals. He will baptize you with the Holy Spirit and with fire. He is ready to separate the chaff from the wheat with his winnowing fork. Then he will clean up the threshing area, gathering the wheat into his barn but burning the chaff with never-ending fire."
                    Matthew 3:11-12, NLT

We have a choice to make: accept the fire of God's Spirit or ultimately have our works burned up with fire. God wants to be the fire within us:

"Then I, myself, will be a protective wall of fire around Jerusalem," says the LORD. *"And I will be the glory inside the city!"'*   Zechariah 2:5, NLT

The Holy Spirit helps us to stay awake spiritually, and His fire preserves us. Fail? Why would we ever utter that word? As a child of the living God, *I Refuse to Fail,* and you can refuse to fail too*!*

CHAPTER 2

LIVING IN HEAVEN ON EARTH

Then God said, "Let us make human be-ings in our image, to be like us. They will reign over the fish in the sea, the birds in the sky, the livestock, all the wild animals on the earth, and the small animals that scurry along the ground." So God cre-ated human beings in his own image. In the image of God he created them; male and female he created them.

Then God blessed them and said, "Be fruitful and multiply. Fill the earth and govern it. Reign over the fish in the sea, the birds in the sky, and all the animals that scurry along the ground."

Then God said, "Look! I have given you
every seed-bearing plant throughout the
earth and all the fruit trees for your food.
And I have given every green plant as
food for all the wild animals, the birds
in the sky, and the small animals that
scurry along the ground—everything
that has life."   Genesis 1:26-30

I have discovered that in order to live
in Heaven here on Earth we must know
the culture of the Kingdom. Every culture
begins as an idea, that idea becomes an
ideology, and that ideology becomes our
philosophy of life. Why? Because our
thinking affects how we live.

What you think or what you fear began
as an idea that you got from someone
somewhere. God wants us to think His
thoughts, and so He has planted an idea
in the heart of men, the culture of the
throne. God decided to create human be-
ings in His own image, and that's what
happened. Then He gave man an exten-
sion of Heaven on Earth, and everything

that He created was put under the rule of mankind.

Sadly, man "messed up" in the garden, and God had to fulfill His plan by sending Jesus to introduce us to another culture, the culture of the Kingdom.

What must I do to live a life of Heaven on Earth? Here are a few keys:

1. YOU MUST POSITION YOURSELF IN THE WORD

Before you migrate to any country or any city, you must know the culture so as to blend in. That is why you want to enhance your level of command of the Word of God. The Word positions you and me on the victory side throughout life:

> *And take the helmet of salvation, and the sword of the Spirit, which is the word of God.* Ephesians 6:17, KJV

Beloved, your enslavement will continue until the Sword of the Spirit is engaged. It is so very easy to put the enemy out of your jurisdiction by the Word of God.

Jesus said:

> *It is written, Man shall not live by bread alone, but by every word that proceedeth out of the mouth of God.*
>
> Matthew 4:4, KJV

No enemy is permitted to stand against you when you are in the Word and the Word is in you. Yes, God plants the culture of Heaven in the hearts of all believers here on Earth by giving them His Word. He said:

> *And you must commit yourselves wholeheartedly to these commands that I am giving you today. Repeat them again and again to your children. Talk about them when you are at home and when you are on the road, when you are going to bed and when you are getting up. Tie them to your hands and wear them on your forehead as reminders.*

Write them on the doorposts of your house and on your gates.

Deuteronomy 6:6-9

See what God said in the very first chapter of the book of John:

In the beginning was the Word, and the Word was with God, and the Word was God.

In him was life; and the life was the light of men. And the light shineth in darkness; and the darkness comprehended it not. John 1:1 and 4-5, KJV

The darkness tries but cannot understand light because it carries the life that is in God, and the life that is in God cannot be extinguished.

The Bible says in Proverbs:

My son, attend to my words; incline thine ear unto my sayings.

Let them not depart from thine eyes; keep them in the midst of thine heart.

45

For they are life unto those that find them, and health to all their flesh.

Proverbs 4:20-22, KJV

Let me tell you this: your shout can never frighten the devil. It is the Word of God that scares him. Get firmly rooted in the Word, and you will be failure proof.

The Message Translation renders Joshua 1:8 this way:

And don't for a minute let this Book of The Revelation be out of mind. Ponder and meditate on it day and night, making sure you practice everything written in it. Then you'll get where you're going; then you'll succeed.

The Word of God is designed to connect you to the realm of God, and when you enter that realm of results it humbles the world. The Word actually makes you a god:

If he called them gods, unto whom the word of God came, and the scripture cannot be broken; John 10:35, KJV

It is the Word that you receive that makes you a god. Look at how powerful Jesus was through the Word:

That evening many demon-possessed people were brought to Jesus. He cast out the evil spirits with a simple command, and he healed all the sick. This fulfilled the word of the Lord through the prophet Isaiah, who said, "He took our sicknesses and removed our diseases." Matthew 8:16-17

According to the culture of Heaven, you, too, just need a simple command to send away what you don't want around you. Many troublesome things are just waiting for your command to go. One step of faith will send them away, and they *will* obey you.

Beloved, your destiny has been predetermined in God's Word. There is a mystery to speaking the Word in faith, and you can do it when you are determined not to miss the mark.

We live in a world full of cruelty on the part of the enemy, but the Word of God brings us into a place of rulership.

The Bible spoke about the Berean Christians this way:

> *These were more fair-minded than those in Thessalonica, in that they received the word with all readiness, and searched the Scriptures daily to find out whether these things were so.*
> Acts 17:11, NKJV

John concluded:

> *This is the message we heard from Jesus and now declare to you: God is light, and there is no darkness in him at all. So we are lying if we say we have fellowship with God but go on living in spiritual darkness; we are not practicing the truth.* 1 John 1:5-6

The Word of God declares you to be a world changer, an agent of change everywhere you go.

2. YOU MUST DISCOVER WHO YOU ARE IN CHRIST

Always remember, John 5:39 says that when you search the Scriptures you know that you have eternal life. I have found that discovering your true self in Christ makes a life of wonder your present reality. To have success in life, you must be able to understand your identity in God.

When someone asked Jesus who He was, He had a ready answer:

> *"Who are you?" they demanded.*
> *Jesus replied, "The one I have always claimed to be."* John 8:25

Jesus knew who He was. In verse 23, He said:

*"You are from below; I am from above.
You belong to this world; I do not."*
                                        John 8:23

Jesus was saying, "What is happening here cannot happen to Me. What is killing them cannot kill Me. What is afflicting them cannot afflict Me." Why? Because He was *"from above."*

John 3:31 records:

For the one who is from the earth belongs to the earth and speaks from the natural realm. But the One who comes from above is above everything and speaks of the highest realm of all! (TPT)

Beloved, the warfare many believers are fighting every day is a warfare of identity. Let me help you:

- According to Romans 8:17, you are an heir of God and a joint heir with Christ.
- According to Philippians 3:20, you are a citizen of Heaven, where the Lord Jesus Himself lives.

- According to Romans 8:16, you are an ambassador of Christ and, therefore, must enjoy the same experience as your home country. Paul declared:

And the same one who descended is the one who ascended higher than all the heavens, so that he might fill the entire universe with himself.

Ephesians 4:10

Since we have been united with him in his death, we will also be raised to life as he was.

For when we died with Christ we were set free from the power of sin. And since we died with Christ, we know we will also live with him. We are sure of this because Christ was raised from the dead, and he will never die again. Death no longer has any power over him.

When he died, he died once to break the power of sin. But now that he lives, he lives for the glory of God. So you also should consider yourselves to be dead to the power of sin and alive to God through Christ Jesus.

Romans 6:5, and 7-11

I am writing to all of you in Rome who are loved by God and are called to be his own holy people. May God our Father and the Lord Jesus Christ give you grace and peace. Romans 1:7

Yet now he has reconciled you to himself through the death of Christ in his physical body. As a result, he has brought you into his own presence, and you are holy and blameless as you stand before him without a single fault. But you must continue to believe this truth and stand firmly in it. Don't drift away from the assurance you received when you heard the Good News. The Good News has been preached all over the world, and I, Paul, have been appointed as God's servant to proclaim it.

Colossians 1:22-23

John's writings agree:

And God has given us his Spirit as proof that we live in him and he in us. Furthermore, we have seen with our own eyes and now testify that the Father sent his Son to be the Savior of the world. All who declare that Jesus is the Son of God have God living in them, and they live in God.

And as we live in God, our love grows more perfect. So we will not be afraid on the day of judgment, but we can face him with confidence because we live like Jesus here in this world.

1 John 4:13-15 and 17

Paul wrote to the Philippian believers:

But we are a colony of heaven on earth as we cling tightly to our life-giver, the Lord Jesus Christ.

Philippians 3:20, TPT

This is all part of the born-again experience. Jesus said:

> *"I tell you the truth, unless you are born again, you cannot see the Kingdom of God."*
> *"I assure you, no one can enter the Kingdom of God without being born of water and the Spirit. Humans can reproduce only human life, but the Holy Spirit gives birth to spiritual life. So don't be surprised when I say, 'You must be born again.' The wind blows wherever it wants. Just as you can hear the wind but can't tell where it comes from or where it is going, so you can't explain how people are born of the Spirit."*   John 3:3 and 5-8

In his first letter to the churches, John wrote:

> *And God has given us his Spirit as proof that we live in him and he in us. Furthermore, we have seen with our*

own eyes and now testify that the Father sent his Son to be the Savior of the world. All who declare that Jesus is the Son of God have God living in them, and they live in God. We know how much God loves us, and we have put our trust in his love. God is love, and all who live in love live in God, and God lives in them. And as we live in God, our love grows more perfect. So we will not be afraid on the day of judgment, but we can face him with confidence because we live like Jesus here in this world.

1 John 4:13-17

Fail? Why would we ever utter that word? As a child of the living God, *I Refuse to Fail,* and you can refuse to fail too*!*

CHAPTER 3

BECOMING UNMOVABLE

Therefore, my beloved brethren, be ye stedfast, UNMOVEABLE, always abounding in the work of the Lord, for-asmuch as ye know that your labour is not in vain in the Lord.

1 Corinthians 15:58, KJV
(My Emphasis)

This is what God says about you. You can be steadfast and unmovable. He says you can always abound in the work of the Lord. If you choose to ignore His words, you can, but anyone who will listen can never be the same again.

I have found that a lot of women are dying in silence these days. Some of them are depressed and oppressed, and they feel they cannot share what they are suffering for fear of betrayal. If that is your case, this chapter is for you. You can be steadfast and unmovable. Here are some keys to enjoying peace in the midst of every storm:

1. BE UNMOVABLE BY TRUSTING GOD

A SONG OF THE STAIRWAY

Those who trust in the LORD are as unshakeable,
as unmovable as mighty Mount Zion!
Just as the mountains surround Jerusalem,
so the LORD's wrap-around presence surrounds his people,
protecting them now and forever.

Psalm 125:1-2, TPT

As you learn to trust God, you will see that He cannot be shaken, and because you are in Him, you are also unshakable:

Let us hold tightly without wavering to the hope we affirm, for God can be trusted to keep his promise.

Hebrews 10:23

What do I need to do to show that I trust God? I can prove my trust in Him by holding *"tightly without wavering to the hope we affirm."* What is *"the hope we affirm"*? It is the hope that our God has a Kingdom that is unshakable, and when I am holding tightly to that hope, I too cannot be shaken.

This is confirmed by many scriptures:

Since we are receiving a Kingdom that is unshakable, let us be thankful and please God by worshiping him with holy fear and awe. Hebrews 12:28

So now, beloved ones, stand firm and secure. Live your lives with an unshakable confidence. We know that we prosper and excel in every season by serving the Lord, because we are assured that our

*union with the Lord makes our labor
productive with fruit that endures.*
1 Corinthians 15:58, TPT

How and where can I obtain such unshakable confidence? From God's Word. Those who hear God's voice above the noise of men cannot fail.

Judges 4 tells the story of two great and powerful women. One of them was Deborah, the great judge over Israel, and the other was a lesser known woman named Jael. Through this relatively unknown woman, God gave a great victory to the Israelites.

One day Sisera, a Canaanite commander who had cruelly oppressed the Israelites for twenty years, sought refuge from battle in Jael's tent. She welcomed him in and gave him a place to rest. He asked her to guard the door and make sure no one came in to do him harm, but she had other plans. When Sisera had fallen into a deep sleep, Jael took it upon herself to kill him with her own hands. The chapter ends with these powerful words:

So on that day Israel saw God defeat Jabin, the Canaanite king [Sisera's master]. From that time on Israel became stronger and stronger against King Jabin until they finally destroyed him. Judges 4:23-24

It all began with a valiant woman of faith named Jael. Beloved, you will never know what God can do through you until you give Him a chance to prove it.

Remember that desperate widow from Chapter 1? One minute her situation seemed hopeless, and the next minute her needs were all met. Why?

So she did as she was told. Her sons kept bringing jars to her, and she filled one after another. 2 Kings 4:5

"She did as she was told." Your strength also lies in doing what God has asked you to do. He has declared that you can be immovable, and if He said it, you can do it as you hear His voice and are obedient to Him.

2. BE UNMOVABLE BY KNOWING THAT YOUR LABOR IS NOT IN VAIN

No, your labor is never in vain when you are in the Lord:

They will not work in vain,
and their children will not be doomed
to misfortune.
For they are people blessed by the LORD,
and their children, too, will be blessed.
                                    Isaiah 65:23

Have you experienced so much for noth-
ing? Surely it was not in vain, was it?
                                    Galatians 3:4

Hold firmly to the word of life; then,
on the day of Christ's return, I will be
proud that I did not run the race in vain
and that my work was not useless.
                                    Philippians 2:16

When you are walking with Christ, noth-ing is ever in vain.

3. Be Unmovable by Your Praise

When you know the goodness of God, praise comes naturally and becomes a protection over your life:

> *In every thing give thanks: for this is the will of God in Christ Jesus concerning you.*
> 1 Thessalonians 5:18, KJV

> *In that wonderful day you will sing:*
> *"Thank the Lord! Praise his name!*
> *Tell the nations what he has done.*
> *Let them know how mighty he is!*
> Isaiah 12:4

> *Praise the Lord from the earth,*
> *you creatures of the ocean depths,*
> *fire and hail, snow and clouds,*
> *wind and weather that obey him,*
> *mountains and all hills,*
> *fruit trees and all cedars,*
> *wild animals and all livestock,*
> *small scurrying animals and birds,*

kings of the earth and all people,
rulers and judges of the earth,
young men and young women,
old men and children.
Let them all praise the name of the Lord.
For his name is very great;
his glory towers over the earth and
heaven!
He has made his people strong,
honoring his faithful ones—
the people of Israel who are close to him.
Praise the Lord*!*   Psalm 148:7-14

4. Be Unmovable by Your Knowledge of God's Promises

Now all of us can come to the Father
through the same Holy Spirit because
of what Christ has done for us.
Ephesians 2:18

So the Word became human and made
his home among us. He was full of
unfailing love and faithfulness. And

64

we have seen his glory, the glory of the Father's one and only Son.

John 1:14

From his abundance we have all received one gracious blessing after another.

John 1:16

So we have not stopped praying for you since we first heard about you. We ask God to give you complete knowledge of his will and to give you spiritual wisdom and understanding. Then the way you live will always honor and please the Lord, and your lives will produce every kind of good fruit. All the while, you will grow as you learn to know God better and better. Colossians 1:9-10

Look, I have given you authority over all the power of the enemy, and you can walk among snakes and scorpions and crush them. Nothing will injure you.

Luke 10:19

These miraculous signs will accompany those who believe: They will cast out demons in my name, and they will speak in new languages. Mark 16:17

Because of the covenant I made with you,
sealed with blood,
I will free your prisoners from death in a waterless dungeon.
Come back to the place of safety,
all you prisoners who still have hope!
I promise this very day
that I will repay two blessings for each of your troubles. Zechariah 9:11-12

Look around you and see,
for all your children will come back to you.
As surely as I live," says the LORD,
"they will be like jewels or bridal ornaments for you to display."
Isaiah 49:18

66

5. BE UNMOVABLE BY YOUR OBEDIENCE

Those who reject Christ cannot hope to receive His favor:

> *But his people hated him and sent a delegation after him to say, "We do not want him to be our king."*
>
> Luke 19:14

> *It will be called the Land of Nothing, and all its nobles will soon be gone. Thorns will overrun its palaces; nettles and thistles will grow in its forts. The ruins will become a haunt for jackals and a home for owls. Desert animals will mingle there with hyenas, their howls filling the night. Wild goats will bleat at one another among the ruins, and night creatures will come there to rest.* Isaiah 34:12-14

67

God is looking for faithful children that He can bless:

Before he left, he called together ten of his servants and divided among them ten pounds of silver, saying, "Invest this for me while I am gone." Luke 19:13

Pray like this: Our Father in heaven, may your name be kept holy. May your Kingdom come soon. May your will be done on earth, as it is in heaven.
Matthew 6:9-10

Soldiers don't get tied up in the affairs of civilian life, for then they cannot please the officer who enlisted them. And athletes cannot win the prize unless they follow the rules. And hardworking farmers should be the first to enjoy the fruit of their labor. Think about what I am saying. The Lord will help you understand all these things.
2 Timothy 2:4-7

5. Be Unmovable through the Anointing of the Holy Spirit

God anointed Jesus for His work on Earth:

And you know that God anointed Jesus of Nazareth with the Holy Spirit and with power. Then Jesus went around doing good and healing all who were oppressed by the devil, for God was with him. Acts 10:38

The disciples of Jesus were anointed in the same way as Jesus was:

Even as Peter was saying these things, the Holy Spirit fell upon all who were listening to the message. Acts 10:44

It is up to us to seek God and to live in such a way as to invite the anointing of His Spirit:

Because we have these promises, dear friends, let us cleanse ourselves from

69

everything that can defile our body or spirit. And let us work toward complete holiness because we fear God.

2 Corinthians 7:1

God is faithful to you. Are you faithful to Him?

I have sworn by my own name;
I have spoken the truth,
and I will never go back on my word:
Every knee will bend to me,
and every tongue will declare allegiance
to me. "   Isaiah 45:23

Having done these things, you will become unmovable and will never fail. Fail? Why would we ever utter that word? As a child of the living God, *I Refuse to Fail,* and you can refuse to fail too!

THE FAVOR OF GOD
IS UPON ME NOW

The Spirit of the Sovereign Lord is upon me,

for the Lord has anointed me

to bring good news to the poor.

He has sent me to comfort the brokenhearted

and to proclaim that captives will be released

and prisoners will be freed.

He has sent me to tell those who mourn

that the time of the Lord's favor has come,

and with it, the day of God's anger against their enemies.   Isaiah 61:1-2

Life is good and it is planned. The Owner put everything in place before inviting us to come. Beloved, before God ever spoke the words, *"Let there be light,"* setting in motion the creation of all that exists, He had a marvelous plan for all of mankind.

No destiny fulfills itself; it is people who fulfill destiny. Consider the following passages:

The LORD of hosts shall defend and protect them;
And they will devour [the enemy] and trample down the slingstones [that have missed their mark],
And they will drink [of victory] and be boisterous as with wine;
And they shall be filled like sacrificial bowls [used to catch the blood],
Drenched like the corners of the [sacrificial] altar.
And the LORD their God shall save them on that day
As the flock of His people;
For they are like the [precious] jewels of a crown,

Displayed and glittering in His land.
For how great is God's goodness and how great is His beauty!
And how great [He will make Israel's goodliness and [Israel's] beauty!
Grain and new wine will make the young men and virgins flourish.
Zechariah 9:15-17, AMP

The Message Bible says it this way:

Then God will come into view,
his arrows flashing like lightning!
Master God will blast his trumpet
and set out in a whirlwind.
God-of-the-Angel-Armies will protect them —
all-out war,
The war to end all wars,
no holds barred.
Their God will save the day.
He'll rescue them.
They'll become like sheep, gentle and soft,
Or like gemstones in a crown,
catching all the colors of the sun.

73

*Then how they'll shine! shimmer! glow!
the young men robust, the young
women lovely!*

Zechariah 9:14-17, MSG

As Paul wrote in his letter to the Galatians,
God's plan was for all people to be blessed:

*What's more, the Scriptures looked for-
ward to this time when God would make
the Gentiles right in his sight because of
their faith. God proclaimed this good news
to Abraham long ago when he said, "All
nations will be blessed through you." So
all who put their faith in Christ share the
same blessing Abraham received because
of his faith.* Galatians 3:8-9

*But Christ has rescued us from the curse
pronounced by the law. When he was
hung on the cross, he took upon himself the curse for our wrongdoing. For
it is written in the Scriptures, "Cursed
is everyone who is hung on a tree."
Through Christ Jesus, God has blessed*

the Gentiles with the same blessing he promised to Abraham, so that we who are believers might receive the promised Holy Spirit through faith.

God gave the promises to Abraham and his child. And notice that the Scripture doesn't say "to his children," as if it meant many descendants. Rather, it says "to his child"—and that, of course, means Christ.

And now that you belong to Christ, you are the true children of Abraham. You are his heirs, and God's promise to Abraham belongs to you.

Galatians 3:13-14, 16, and 29

That promise is mine too. How about you?

Through our union with Christ we too have been claimed by God as his own inheritance. Before we were even born, he gave us our destiny; that we would fulfill the plan of God who always accomplishes every purpose and plan in his heart. Ephesians 1:11, TPT

So the promise is received by faith. It is given as a free gift. And we are all certain to receive it, whether or not we live according to the law of Moses, if we have faith like Abraham's. For Abraham is the father of all who believe.

Romans 4:16

Favor is something you don't work for, and having a Kingdom mindset about favor will make you and me to know that we already have favor without doing anything to earn it. You didn't pay for the air you breath, and you didn't pay for the use of God's seas. God saw that we needed them and made them available to us.

Just as a password gives you access to a computer program, faith enables you to walk in God's unmerited favor. And faith has nothing to do with what you do or what you can do. Faith is simply believing and declaring what God has done and is doing for you.

When you believe that the favor of God is on you because of Christ's finished work, His promises of provision, healing, and restoration become sure to you. They are not just sure to the Jews, but also to you and me. Why? Because we are *"of the faith of Abraham."*

Ruth was a Gentile widow who put her faith in God's grace. She believed and declared that God's favor would lead her to the right field in which to glean, where she would find favor in the owner's sight (see Ruth 2:2). Because she depended on God's unmerited favor, God not only placed her in the field of a wealthy man, Boaz, but she also became part of the genealogy of Jesus (see Matthew 1:5).

Ruth's faith in God's favor opened up a whole new world for her. She went from poverty to supply, from widowhood to marriage, and from being childless to having a complete family. She also became a respected member of the community (see Ruth 4:13-15).

If Ruth, a Gentile who was under the old covenant, enjoyed God's favor, how much more will we, who are under the new covenant of grace, enjoy the blessings that the unmerited favor of God bring! In fact, God sees us as part of the Beloved today, and we enjoy the same favor that Jesus had when He walked the Earth (see Ephesians 1:3-6).

My friend, when you believe that you have the same favor that Jesus had, a whole new world will open up to you—a world where all of God's promises are "Yes" and "Amen" in Christ (see 2 Corinthians 1:20).

> *How blessed and graciously favored is he whose help is the God of Jacob (Israel),*
> *Whose hope is in the LORD his God,*
> *Who made heaven and earth,*
> *The sea, and all that is in them,*
> *Who keeps truth and is faithful forever.*
> Psalm 146:5-6, AMP

To favor someone is to endorse them. It also means to support or assist. The Bible says:

> *Therefore, angels are only servants-spirits sent to care for people who will inherit salvation.* Hebrews 1:14

That is heavenly support and assistance. God said to the children of Israel in the wilderness:

"See, I am sending an angel before you to protect you on your journey and lead you safely to the place I have prepared for you. Pay close attention to him, and obey his instructions. Do not rebel against him, for he is my representative, and he will not forgive your rebellion. But if you are careful to obey him, following all my instructions, then I will be an enemy to your enemies, and I will oppose those who oppose you."

Exodus 23:20-22

Favor makes things easier, giving you sweat-free victories. Favor is the mighty hand of God stretched out in mercy to bring a man or woman to His purpose. That hand will locate you today. The reason your enemies will fail this year and you won't is that the favor of God is upon your life:

*By this I know that You favor and de-
light in me,*
*Because my enemy does not shout in
triumph over me.* Psalm 41:11, AMP

*Now God granted Daniel favor and com-
passion in the sight of the commander of
the officials, and the commander of the
officials said to Daniel, "I am afraid of
my lord the king, who has prearranged
your food and your drink; for why
should he see your faces looking more
haggard than the young men who are
your own age? Then you would make
me forfeit my head to the king."*
*But Daniel said to the overseer whom
the commander of the officials had
appointed over Daniel, Hananiah,
Mishael, and Azariah, "Please, test
your servants for ten days, and let us be
given some vegetables to eat and water
to drink. Then let our appearance and
the appearance of the young men who
eat the king's finest food be observed
and compared by you, and deal with*

*your servants in accordance with what
you see."*

*So the man listened to them in this mat-
ter and tested them for ten days. At the
end of ten days it seemed that they were
looking better and healthier than all the
young men who ate the king's finest
food.* Daniel 1:9-15, AMP

That is what God's favor will do. That is
why I know what Job also learned:

*When men are cast down, then thou shalt
say, There is lifting up; and he shall save
the humble person.* Job 22:29, KJV

The story of Daniel continues:

*So the overseer continued to withhold
their fine food and the wine they were to
drink, and kept giving them vegetables.
As for these four young men, God gave
them knowledge and skill in all kinds of
literature and wisdom; Daniel also understood all kinds of visions and dreams.*

At the end of the time set by the king to bring all the young men in [before him], the commander of the officials presented them to Nebuchadnezzar.

Daniel 1:16-18, AMP

That is God's favor.

The LORD delivers;
you show favor to your people. (Selah)

Psalm 3:8, NET

If the grace of God or the favor of God is on you, then the presence of God is with you as well. We see this in Exodus:

And the LORD said unto Moses, Depart, and go up hence, thou and the people which thou hast brought up out of the land of Egypt, unto the land which I sware unto Abraham, to Isaac, and to Jacob, saying, Unto thy seed will I give it: and I will send an angel before thee; and I will drive out the Canaanite, the Amorite, and the

Hittite, and the Perizzite, the Hivite, and the Jebusite: unto a land flowing with milk and honey: for I will not go up in the midst of thee; for thou art a stiffnecked people: lest I consume thee in the way.

And when the people heard these evil tidings, they mourned: and no man did put on him his ornaments. For the Lord *had said unto Moses, Say unto the children of Israel, Ye are a stiffnecked people: I will come up into the midst of thee in a moment, and consume thee: therefore now put off thy ornaments from thee, that I may know what to do unto thee.*

And the Lord *spake unto Moses face to face, as a man speaketh unto his friend. And he turned again into the camp: but his servant Joshua, the son of Nun, a young man, departed not out of the tabernacle. And Moses said unto the* Lord*, See, thou sayest unto me, Bring up this people: and thou hast not let me know whom thou wilt send with* *me. Yet thou hast said, I know thee by name, and thou hast also found grace in my sight. Now therefore, I pray thee, if I have found grace in thy sight, shew me now thy way, that I may know thee, that I may find grace in thy sight: and consider that this nation is thy people. And he said, My presence shall go with thee, and I will give thee rest.*

And he said unto him, If thy presence go not with me, carry us not up hence. For wherein shall it be known here that I and thy people have found grace in thy sight? is it not in that thou goest with us? so shall we be separated, I and thy people, from all the people that are upon the face of the earth.

And the Lord *said unto Moses, I will do this thing also that thou hast spoken: for thou hast found grace in my sight, and I know thee by name.*

And he said, I will make all my goodness pass before thee, and I will proclaim the name of the Lord *before thee; and will be gracious to whom I*

*will be gracious, and will shew mercy
on whom I will shew mercy.*
        Exodus 33:1-5,11-17 and 19, KJV

The only reason we are alive today is that
the favor of God allows us to live. He has
graced us to exist. Thank God!

Beloved, the secret of Jesus' triumph on
Earth was the favor of His Father:

*And Jesus kept increasing in wisdom
and in stature, and in favor with God
and men.*   Luke 2:52, AMP

The New Living Translation says it this
way:

*Jesus grew in wisdom and in stature
and in favor with God and all the people.*

The apostles, the followers of Jesus, also
enjoyed favor from God:

*Praising God continually, and having
favor with all the people. And the Lord*

kept adding to their number daily those who were being saved.

Acts 2:47, AMP

Favor brought constant increase to their lives. When the favor of God is upon you, no adversary will be able to stop you from moving forward. You are moving in the name of Jesus and by His authority:

Now a new king arose over Egypt, who did not know Joseph [nor the history of his accomplishments]. He said to his people, "Behold, the people of the sons of Israel are too many and too mighty for us [they greatly outnumber us]. Come, let us deal shrewdly with them, so that they will not multiply and in the event of war, join our enemies, and fight against us and escape from the land." So they set taskmasters over them to oppress them with hard labor.

And the sons of Israel built Pithom and Raamses as storage cities for Pharaoh.

86

*But the more the Egyptians oppressed
them, the more they multiplied and ex-
panded, so that the Egyptians dreaded
and were exasperated by the Israelites.*
                                    Exodus 1:8-12, AMP

Beloved, when the favor of God is on you,
you are on your way to the top:

*For You are the glory of their strength
[their proud adornment],
And by Your favor our horn is exalted.*
                                    Psalm 89:17, AMP

Since God's favor does so much for us,
what are some things I can do to provoke
that favor over my life? For one, provoke
God's favor through prayer.

Yes, prayer can provoke God's favor upon
your life. The Bible shows us:

*Behold, as the eyes of servants look to
the hand of their master,
And as the eyes of a maid to the hand of
her mistress,*

So our eyes look to the LORD our God,
Until He is gracious and favorable to-
ward us.
Be gracious to us, O LORD, be gracious
and favorable toward us,
For we are greatly filled with contempt.
                              Psalm 123:2-3, AMP

Yes, it's time for you to manifest God's favor in your everyday life:

And let the [gracious] favor of the LORD
our God be on us;
Confirm for us the work of our hands—
Yes, confirm the work of our hands.
                              Psalm 90:17, AMP

In the days to come, you will not struggle at all. The works of your hands will be approved by God. Let's us see this in the Scriptures:

For in this city there were gathered
together against Your holy Servant
Jesus, whom You anointed, both Herod

and Pontius Pilate, along with the Gentiles and the peoples of Israel, to do whatever Your hand and Your purpose predestined [before the creation of the world] to occur [and so without knowing it, they served Your own purpose]. And now, Lord, observe their threats [take them into account] and grant that Your bond-servants may declare Your message [of salvation] with great confidence, while You extend Your hand to heal, and signs and wonders (attesting miracles) take place through the name [and the authority and power] of Your holy Servant and Son Jesus."

And when they had prayed, the place where they were meeting together was shaken [a sign of God's presence]; and they were all filled with the Holy Spirit and began to speak the word of God with boldness and courage.

Now the company of believers was of one heart and soul, and not one [of them] claimed that anything belonging to him was [exclusively] his own, but everything was common property and for the use of all. And with great ability and power the apostles were continuously testifying to the resurrection of the Lord Jesus, and great grace [God's remarkable lovingkindness and favor and goodwill] rested richly upon them all. Acts 4:27-33, AMP

Righteous lips are the delight of kings, And he who speaks right is loved. Proverbs 16:13, AMP

When a man's ways please the Lord, He makes even his enemies to be at peace with him. Proverbs 16:7, AMP

And He who sent Me is [always] with Me; He has not left Me alone, because I always do what pleases Him. John 8:29, AMP

But grow [spiritually mature] in the grace and knowledge of our Lord and

Savior Jesus Christ. To Him be glory (honor, majesty, splendor), both now and to the day of eternity. Amen.
2 Peter 3:18, AMP

- FAVOR produces supernatural increase and promotion (see Genesis 39:21).
- FAVOR produces restoration of everything that the enemy has stolen from you (see Exodus 3:21).
- FAVOR produces honor in the midst of your adversaries (see Exodus 11:3).
- FAVOR produces increased assets, especially in the area of real estate (see Deuteronomy 33:23).
- FAVOR produces great victories in the midst of great impossibilities (see Joshua 11:20).
- FAVOR produces recognition, even when you seem the least likely to receive it (see 1 Samuel 16:22).
- FAVOR produces prominence and preferential treatment (see Esther 2:17).
- FAVOR produces petitions granted, even by ungodly civil authorities (see Esther 5).

- FAVOR causes policies, rules, regulations, and laws to be changed and reversed to your advantage (see Esther 8:5).
- FAVOR produces battles won, which you won't even fight, because God will fight them for you.

O God, we have heard it with our own ears—our ancestors have told us of all you did in their day, in days long ago: You drove out the pagan nations by your power and gave all the land to our ancestors. You crushed their enemies and set our ancestors free. They did not conquer the land with their swords; it was not their own strong arm that gave them victory. It was your right hand and strong arm and the blinding light from your face that helped them, for you loved them. Psalm 44:1-3

Fail? Why would we ever utter that word? As a child of the living God, *I Refuse to Fail,* and you can refuse to fail too*!*

The Favor of God Is Upon Me Now

CHAPTER 5

LIVING FOR WHAT YOU WERE CREATED FOR

For to me, living means living for Christ, and dying is even better.
                    Philippians 1:21

Life will not add to you what you have deprived yourself of through ignorance. The master plan that sent you here did not expire with your birth. It will be in effect until you see Christ in Glory. It is, therefore, your input that will determine your output:

And I know that whatever God does is final. Nothing can be added to it or taken from it. God's purpose is that people should fear him. What is happening now has happened before, and what will happen in the future has happened before, because God makes the same things happen over and over again.

Ecclesiastes 3:14-15

History merely repeats itself. It has all been done before. Nothing under the sun is truly new. Ecclesiastes 1:9

Beloved, I want you to approach every situation of life with these words, "Dad, whatever You say or do is final."

What else did God say about it?

For every child of God defeats this evil world, and we achieve this victory through our faith. And who can win this battle against the world? Only those who believe that Jesus is the Son of God. 1 John 5:4-5

Do you believe? Then you have achieved your victory. The problem too many believers have is accepting God's Word exactly as it is written. How can I enjoy victory every single day? By knowing more and more about our mighty God and His works. That includes Him creating you. Genesis 1:31 says:

> *Then God looked over all that he had made, and it was excellent in every way. This ended the sixth day.* (TLB)

"It was excellent in every way." The King James Version of the Bible says, *"Behold, it was very good."* That statement ends with a period. That's it. Nothing should be added to nor taken from God's declaration. Any addition is one that you have invited by your acts or choices, and God will never interfere with your right to choose.

If failure, barrenness, miscarriages, or poverty were built into you, God would not have said that you were excellent in every way. When are you going to rebel against those attachments that destabilize you from fulfilling your true destiny?

Neither Satan nor his agents are permitted to add any weight to your life. What do I mean by "weight"? Sickness is a weight, poverty is a weight, and unemployment is a weight. Anything that is burdensome to you is a weight, and our covenant with God forbids such weights.

Your life is so perfectly and excellently built that God forbids that it be rebuilt. From every quarter, no enemy from the pits of Hell can take anything from what God has invested in you. Why? God said it was so that men would fear before Him.

The writer of the Hebrews added:

> *Therefore, since we are surrounded by such a huge crowd of witnesses to the life of faith, let us strip off every weight that slows us down, especially the sin that so easily trips us up. And let us run with endurance the race God has set before us.* Hebrews 12:1

How do we run this race? Verse 2 declares the answer:

We do this by keeping our eyes on Jesus, the champion who initiates and perfects our faith. Because of the joy awaiting him, he endured the cross, disregarding its shame. Now he is seated in the place of honor beside God's throne.

Hebrews 12:2

God is not in feelings, and He is not in fleshly dreams or experiences. God is in faith, as the Bible clearly states.

The greatest crime known to man is to distort the Word of God. That's like destroying God's testimony. Where men have added to it or removed from it, let them be destroyed in the name of Jesus.

How can I maintain my victory through faith?

1. BE SENSITIVE TO YOUR REDEMPTIVE RIGHTS IN CHRIST

Redemption was God plan, and its results satisfy the heart of God and meet every need of man. Christianity links us with God.

And if we are in union with God, then we are successful. Why? Because the mightiest forces in the Universe are at our disposal. The ability of God is our heritage.

Jesus gave a great promise in Acts 1:8:

> *But you will receive power when the Holy Spirit has come upon you; and you shall be My witnesses both in Jerusalem and in all Judea, and Samaria, and as far as the remotest part of the earth.* (NKJV)

The power Jesus was speaking of is the ability of God. Therefore, He was saying, "You shall receive My ability when the Holy Spirit has come upon you." Yes, God's ability is at our disposal. His ability is our inheritance. Peter wrote to the early churches:

> *By his divine power, God has given us everything we need for living a godly life. We have received all of this by coming to know him, the one who called us to himself by means of his marvelous glory and excellence. And because of*

his glory and excellence, he has given us great and precious promises. These are the promises that enable you to share his divine nature and escape the world's corruption caused by human desires.

In view of all this, make every effort to respond to God's promises. Supplement your faith with a generous provision of moral excellence, and moral excellence with knowledge, and knowledge with self-control, and self-control with pa-tient endurance, and patient endurance with godliness. 2 Peter 1:3-6

I once heard the story of a wealthy lady and her maid. In time, the lady reached the end of her life, and her will was opened and read. The will stated that those who had been managing her accounts should con-tinue doing so, and a book was to be given to the faithful maid.

With this, the maid was very angry. "After all these years of my faithful service, the only thing you could give me is a book? You are so wicked!" she said in disgust. She had nowhere to go, so she spoke with the estate manager, and he agreed that she could work for him. So life went on, but the woman was very bitter.

Much time passed, and one day she decided to open the book her former boss had given her. What could be so special about it? But there she found a letter. Curious, she opened it and read. In this way she learned that her former employer had appreciated her greatly and had specified in the letter: "Everything I have now belongs to you. Take this letter to the estate manager, and receive what is yours." Soon all the dead lady's wealth had been transferred to the former maid's name, and she began to enjoy what had been hers for a long time already.

Now take note: your Father gave you a book. He told you to open it and take the letter inside to the Master of all things and to begin to enjoy your inheritance. He said *"put me in remembrance"* (Isaiah 43:26, KJV). The New Living Translation says:

Let us review the situation together, and you can present your case to prove your innocence.

This takes the winning and victory mentality to a whole next level. God told Joshua:

Study this Book of Instruction continually. Meditate on it day and night so you will be sure to obey everything written in it. Only then will you prosper and succeed in all you do. Joshua 1:8

In 2 Timothy 2:15, the King James Version says, *"Study to shew thyself approved."* The New Living Translation says it this way:

Work hard so you can present yourself to God and receive his approval. Be a good worker, one who does not need to be ashamed and who correctly explains the word of truth.

Without a wining mindset, a champion could well become a looser. With a winning mindset, we cannot lose. Romans 8:31 says:

What shall we say about such wonderful things as these? If God is for us, who can ever be against us?

So, what do you think? With God on our side, how can we lose?

2. FOLLOW THE PRINCIPLES OF THE KINGDOM

There is always a principle that governs every act in this world, and when those principles are strictly followed, the result is inevitable. When an object is thrown into the air, the Law of Gravity says that it will come back down. It is a must. There is always an answer to every problem. You may not see it, but every problem carries with it its own answer.

In an objective questions, where you have an option from A to E, all are not the answer, but there is an answer hidden in the question. You can find the answer to every question of your life today in God and in His Word.

One of the greatest principles of the Kingdom is found in Matthew 7:7-8:

Keep on asking, and you will receive what you ask for. Keep on seeking, and you will find. Keep on knocking, and the door will be opened to you. For everyone who asks, receives. Everyone who seeks, finds. And to everyone who knocks, the door will be opened.   Matthew 7:7-8

I love how the Passion Translation puts it

"Ask, and the gift is yours. Seek, and you'll discover. Knock, and the door will be opened for you. For every persistent one will get what he asks for. Every persistent seeker will discover what he longs for. And everyone who knocks persistently will one day find an open door.   Matthew 7:7-8, TPT

"Ask and it shall be given unto you," the King James Version says. This means there is always a way out of every problem. You are never stranded, no matter what you face, how things look, or how the enemy thinks he has gained ground. You can get out of

that "mess." There is a solution attached to the problem. *"What seems impossible to you is never impossible to God":*

> *Looking straight into their eyes, Jesus replied, "Humanly speaking, no one, because no one can save himself. But what seems impossible to you is never impossible to God!"*
> Matthew 19:26, TPT

Jesus said therefore that with God, all things are possible. You don't have an excuse; you must ignore Satan when he wants you to believe that you're finished. There is no such thing as a hopeless situation. When things are looking very tough, your victory is very near. With God, I am a possibilitarian.

The children of Israel were finally out of bondage. After four hundred and thirty years, Pharaoh has just released them. Then he quickly changed his mind and started pursuing them. Suddenly, before them was the Red Sea, and behind them were

Pharaoh's chariots. In the natural, anyone would have concluded that they were finished. But God said:

I will ... make a way in the wilderness.
Isaiah 43:19, KJV

Their covenant God was still alive, and now He would reveal Himself. If you have read your Bible well, you know that situations in life were not meant to frustrate you:

Everything we could ever need for life and complete devotion to God has already been deposited in us by his divine power. For all this was lavished upon us through the rich experience of knowing him who has called us by name and invited us to come to him through a glorious manifestation of his goodness. As a result of this, he has given you magnificent promises that are beyond all price, so that through the power of these tremendous promises you can experience partnership with the divine nature, by which you have escaped the corrupt desires that are of the world.

So devote yourselves to lavishly supplementing your faith with goodness,

and to goodness add understanding,

and to understanding add the strength of self-control,

and to self-control add patient endurance,

and to patient endurance add godliness,

and to godliness add mercy toward your brothers and sisters,

and to mercy toward others add unending love.

Since these virtues are already planted deep within, and you possess them in abundant supply, they will keep you from being inactive or fruitless in your pursuit of knowing Jesus Christ more intimately.

But if anyone lacks these things, he is blind, constantly closing his eyes to the mysteries of our faith, and forgetting his innocence-for his past sins have been washed away.

For this reason, beloved ones, be eager to confirm and validate that God has invited you to salvation and claimed you as his own. If you do these things, you will never stumble. As a result, the kingdom's gates will open wide to you as God choreographs your triumphant entrance into the eternal kingdom of our Lord and Savior, Jesus the Messiah.

2 Peter 1:3-11, TPT

Fail? Why would we ever utter that word? As a child of the living God, *I Refuse to Fail,* and you can refuse to fail too!

CHAPTER 6

USE YOUR GOD-GIVEN AUTHORITY

Jesus called his twelve disciples together and gave them authority to cast out evil spirits and to heal every kind of disease and illness.   Matthew 10:1

Beloved we've been authorized to walk on top of any and every situation. Far too many are still ignorant of their authority in the Kingdom of God and don't yet have the revelation of Who it is who is backing them up. Theoretically, Christians know they have an Advocate, but many are not sure of His ability. John wrote:

But you belong. The Holy One anointed you, and you all know it. I haven't been writing this to tell you something you don't know, but to confirm the truth you do know, and to remind you that the truth doesn't breed lies.

1 John 2:20-21, MSG

With this scriptures alone, I know that me having authority is not a lie. It's the truth, and all of God's promises are coming to pass in my life because they are truth. Truth doesn't breed lies, so if God gave me authority, that's the truth. The question now is: Am I using my authority continuously?

And that about wraps it up. God is strong, and he wants you strong. So take everything the Master has set out for you, well-made weapons of the best materials. And put them to use so you will be able to stand up to everything the Devil throws your way. This is no afternoon athletic contest that we'll walk away from and forget about in

USE YOUR GOD-GIVEN AUTHORITY

a couple of hours. This is for keeps, a life-or-death fight to the finish against the Devil and all his angels.

Be prepared. You're up against far more than you can handle on your own. Take all the help you can get, every weapon God has issued, so that when it's all over but the shouting you'll still be on your feet. Truth, righteousness, peace, faith, and salvation are more than words. Learn how to apply them. You'll need them throughout your life. God's Word is an indispensable weapon.

Ephesians 6:10-18, MSG

Nothing can contend with the Word of God:

For we have the living Word of God, which is full of energy, and it pierces more sharply than a two-edged sword. It will even penetrate to the very core of our being where soul and spirit, bone and marrow meet! It interprets

*and reveals the true thoughts and se-
cret motives of our hearts.*
Hebrews 4:12, TPT

At the same time, prayer is essential in this ongoing war. Pray hard and pray long. Pray for your brothers and sisters. Keep your eyes open. Help keep each other's spirits up so that no one falls behind or drops out. You must always be ready and never give up, and you will always prevail. Is that your portion today?

Saints, there is no authority without re-sponsibility. You cannot have authority and only use it once or once in a while. A continu-ous flow demands continuous responsibility, to maintain and sustain my authority.

1. YOU NEED FOCUS

When we talk about focus we are talking about your center of interest and attraction. The Word of God must be your focus, your center of interest and attraction, if you are to maintain your authority:

And when He had sent the multitudes away, He went up on the mountain by Himself to pray. Now when evening came, He was alone there. But the boat was now in the middle of the sea, tossed by the waves, for the wind was contrary. Now in the fourth watch of the night Jesus went to them, walking on the sea. And when the disciples saw Him walking on the sea, they were troubled, saying, "It is a ghost!" And they cried out for fear.

But immediately Jesus spoke to them, saying, "Be of good cheer! It is I; do not be afraid."

And Peter answered Him and said, "Lord, if it is You, command me to come to You on the water."

So He said, "Come."

And when Peter had come down out of the boat, he walked on the water to go to Jesus. But when he saw that the wind was boisterous, he was afraid; and beginning to sink he cried out, saying, "Lord, save me!" Matthew 14:23-30, NKJV

What do you see about your health, your finances, your life? Peter was, at first confident and on top of his situation. Then, however, He got his eyes off of Jesus, saw the wind and the waves, and this caused him to begin to doubt. The result was that he began sinking and Jesus had to rescue him.

In order to maintain your God-given authority, you must keep His Word hidden in your heart. It must not depart from your mouth, and you must pay attention to it:

Set your gaze on the path before you.
With fixed purpose, looking straight ahead,
ignore life's distractions.
Watch where you're going!
Stick to the path of truth,
and the road will be safe and smooth before you.
Don't allow yourself to be sidetracked for even a moment
or take the detour that leads to darkness. Proverbs 4:25-27, TPT

Ignore life's distractions so that you can maintain your authority and continue winning. Let the Lord move you *"from glory to glory"*:

> *But we all, with open face beholding as in a glass the glory of the Lord, are changed into the same image from glory to glory, even as by the Spirit of the Lord.* 2 Corinthians 3:18, KJV

Hebrews 3:1 declares:

> *So, my dear Christian friends, companions in following this call to the heights, take a good hard look at Jesus. He's the centerpiece of everything we believe, faithful in everything God gave him to do.* (MSG)

Who you look at is who you will look like. Paul wrote to Timothy:

> *No man that warreth entangleth himself with the affairs of this life; that he may*

117

please him who hath chosen him to be a
soldier. 2 Timothy 2:4, KJV

The writer of Hebrews called for our total focus:

Looking unto Jesus the author and fin-
isher of our faith; who for the joy that
was set before him endured the cross,
despising the shame, and is set down at
the right hand of the throne of God. For
consider him that endured such contra-
diction of sinners against himself, lest
ye be wearied and faint in your minds.
Hebrews 12:2-3, KJV

The Passion Translation renders verse 2 this way:

We look away from the natural realm
and we fasten our gaze onto Jesus who
birthed faith within us and who leads
us forward into faith's perfection. His
example is this: Because his heart was
focused on the joy of knowing that you

would be his, he endured the agony of the cross and conquered its humiliation, and now sits exalted at the right hand of the throne of God!

Hebrews 12:2, TPT

Set your focus on Him and you can't lose. Since nothing can defeat Him, you also cannot be defeated when He is your Light!

2. NEVER GIVE PLACE TO THE DEVIL

In Ephesians 4:27, the Word of the Lord gives us a very short but important key. It says:

Neither give place to the devil. (KJV)

This is so important. James wrote:

Submit yourselves therefore to God. Resist the devil, and he will flee from you. James 4:7, KJV

The Passion Translation says it this way:

So then, surrender to God. Stand up to the devil and resist him and he will turn and run away from you. TPT

The armor of God and many spiritual weapons are at your disposal, and God is there with you to back up His Word. You have the power and the authority to use the Word of God, the name of Jesus, and the power of the Holy Spirit, and in doing so, you can run Satan out of your affairs.

Dont pray and ask God to fight Satan for you. You have the authority. Take responsibility and speak directly to Satan yourself, stand your ground by continuously declaring the Word of God, and the enemy *will* flee.

Jesus said:

For I will give you a mouth and wisdom, which all your adversaries shall not be able to gainsay nor resist.

Luke 21:15, KJV

Do as Paul suggested in 1 Thessalonians 5:17:

Make your life a prayer. (TPT)

The King James Version says *"pray without ceasing."* This was one of the secrets of the success of the early church.

> *After this prayer, the meeting place shook, and they were all filled with the Holy Spirit. Then they preached the word of God with boldness.* Acts 4:31

When you learn to use your God-given authority, you will always win. Fail? Why would we ever utter that word? As a child of the living God, *I Refuse to Fail,* and you can refuse to fail too!

CHAPTER 7

USE YOUR FAITH

The one who is the true light, who gives light to everyone, was coming into the world. He came into the very world he created, but the world didn't recognize him. He came to his own people, and even they rejected him. But to all who believed him and accepted him, he gave the right to become children of God. They are re-born — not with a physical birth resulting from human passion or plan, but a birth that comes from God.   John 1:9-13

I have discovered that Heaven on Earth is impossible without light and without faith.

Faith makes you victorious over every situation that confronts you:

> *The disciples went and woke him up, shouting, "Master, Master, we're going to drown!"*
> *When Jesus woke up, he rebuked the wind and the raging waves. Suddenly the storm stopped and all was calm. Then he asked them, "Where is your faith?"* Luke 8:24-25

It is important to have your faith in control at all times. Faith brings you into the realm of the invisible God so that you can do incredible things:

> *It was by faith that Moses left the land of Egypt, not fearing the king's anger. He kept right on going because he kept his eyes on the one who is invisible.* Hebrews 11:27

The understanding of the love of God for you is your connecting point to the realm of His presence:

Furthermore, because we are united with Christ, we have received an inheritance from God, for he chose us in advance, and he makes everything work out according to his plan.

Ephesians 1:11

Please take note of the following: God only speaks the future, not the present:

That is what the Scriptures mean when God told him, "I have made you the father of many nations." This happened because Abraham believed in the God who brings the dead back to life and who creates new things out of nothing.

Romans 4:17

Start praying results, not questions or problems. Faith may not make sense to the unbeliever, but God is in it. Pay attention to the promises of the Scriptures, not the problem at hand.

That verse in context looks like this:

That is what the Scriptures mean when God told him, "I have made you the father of many nations." This happened because Abraham believed in the God who brings the dead back to life and who creates new things out of nothing. Even when there was no reason for hope, Abraham kept hoping—believing that he would become the father of many nations. For God had said to him, "That's how many descendants you will have!" And Abraham's faith did not weaken, even though, at about 100 years of age, he figured his body was as good as dead—and so was Sarah's womb. Abraham never wavered in believing God's promise. In fact, his faith grew stronger, and in this he brought glory to God. He was fully convinced that God is able to do whatever he promises.

Romans 4:17-21

Look to what God has said, not what you feel. Don't even consider other alternatives.

Those final verses are so powerful:

Abraham never wavered in believing God's promise. In fact, his faith grew stronger, and in this he brought glory to God. He was fully convinced that God is able to do whatever he promises.
Romans 4:20-21

Dont analyze God; just stand upon His Word. Give Him all the glory, and continue to give Him all the glory:

Be thankful in all circumstances, for this is God's will for you who belong to Christ Jesus.   1 Thessalonians 5:18

It is good to give thanks to the LORD, to sing praises to the Most High.
Psalm 92:1

Counting your blessings eliminates the chance of failure. When Satan assails you, shout out: "My faith is working, and I refuse to fail!" Fail? Why would we ever utter that word? As a child of the living God, *I Refuse to Fail,* and based on His promises to you, you can refuse to fail too*!*

Amen!

Other Books by
Rev. Dr. Omolara Idowu

Word Therapy

Making the Word of God Work in Your Life

by
Rev. Dr. Omolara Idowu

AUTHOR CONTACT PAGE

You may contact Rev. Dr. Omolara Idowu in the following ways:

eMail: lirrypop980@gmail.com

Phone: 904-469-5724